Weight

BY DEREK O'NEILL

GW01091206

Dedication

To all who read this book, I salute you for wanting to change the way you live for the better and for having the courage to be who you are as fully as possible.

To all who encourage me everyday to keep going and sharing their lives with me, family small and large. But most of all the little angels who came to teach me – Alexa and Blake, my grandchildren.

"Everybody hurts sometimes, and when we do it is nice to have Derek O'Neill around. His excellent little books on the things that get us, (fear, anger, depression, victimhood, mental blocks) allow us to find our way safely through our psychological minefields and arrive safely at the other side. Read them when you need them."

- Paul Perry, Author of the
New York Times Bestseller
Evidence of the Afterlife

TABLE OF CONTENTS

Author's Preface

Thank you for purchasing *Weight—What's Eating You?* This book has not come about as a result of my training as a therapist, but through some hard-learned lessons that I have experienced myself. This is how I know the path out of limiting beliefs and behaviors that hinder our growth. The tools that I offer in this book have worked not only for me, but also for hundreds, if not thousands, of people. I have shared these ideas in workshops, one-on-one sessions, and on my website. Through observation of myself and others, I have learned to identify the triggers and root causes of disharmony. Most of all, I have come to understand and utilize the best methods to achieve peace and balance again in life; not perfection, but real transformation and harmony that comes with learning who we are and what makes us tick. My 35 years of martial arts study has given me a refined sense of timing for when to strike with the sword to cut away old patterns and beliefs, and when to use the brush to paint the picture in my mind of the life we deserve and can have.

These 'Get a Grip' series of books offer tangible, authentic wisdom that will transform not only your life, but create a system for you that can help with all aspects of your life. You've made a great choice to invest in yourself by buying this book, or series of books. Let's change who we are together.

Derek

WEIGHT

What's Eating You?

Weight on the Mind is Weight in the Body - What's Behind Your Eating Habits?

Overeating, weight gain, difficulty dieting, and the seemingly insurmountable task of keeping the pounds off . . . these are serious challenges, faced by millions of people. Even with all the diets, exercise plans, and therapeutic approaches, we just can't seem to get to the root of our weight problems. What are the issues, feelings and self-image problems that stand in the way of a healthy, balanced and harmonious relationship to food? In order to understand "what's eating you," a careful look into your past, your emotional connections to food, and your overall feeling about yourself are all key to letting go of the weight that has become a shield from the truth. No diet can address the real reason you hold on to extra pounds. It takes a desire to dig deeper, and a commitment to change, in order to confront the issue of weight in a genuine and lasting way.

In my over-20 years of experience as a therapist, the phrase "weight on the mind is weight on the body" has proven to be accurate, again and again. When people have come to see me for assistance with various weight issues, the number on the scale is usually just the "effect." The "cause" is deep-seated and has to do with what we learn growing up, dealing with our family dynamics, and how those patterns play out in our adult lives.

Here's an example: You were sitting at the table as a child, and you wouldn't eat your cabbage (or anything that was green!) Your mother or father said, "Finish your dinner. There are children starving in the world, and you're very lucky to have food!" That's called a double bind statement. No matter how you respond to it, there's negativity assumed in the words. It's a perfect case of "damned if you do, and damned if you don't." Statements like that create a guilt complex. You are guilty if you eat the food after hearing that statement because there are children starving in the world. You're guilty if you don't eat the food because there are children starving in the world.

I've had to untangle powerful statements like that, which produce guilt for many, many people that I've helped with weight issues. Comments and statements that made you feel guilty as a child stay buried, but present, in your adult mind. Going to the gym, dieting and any other work you undertake towards losing weight doesn't address letting go of the shame that was formed years before. There may be temporary control over the weight, but something will trigger those double bind statements, criticisms or negative reinforcements, and the pounds will start to come back (and sometimes with friends, called "extra pounds.") We need to address those issues in order to understand how "weight on the mind is weight on the body" manifests in your life.

In the following pages, we'll take a unique look at what's behind the relationship between weight, past experiences and the subconscious. Our self-image is formed by many factors, and when we internalize negative messages and events, our ability to take care of ourselves in a healthy, loving way is affected. Traumas, whether spread out over our childhood in the form of a critical parent, or an extreme situation as in the case of sexual abuse, can have a direct connection to the struggle with weight. Extra pounds often come to represent the protection and cover that we want from hurt. Even when we know that the weight is a symptom, often substituting something we felt we lost or were harmed by, it can be so difficult to take the next step and break the patterns. Weight can feel "safe," though in reality, it keeps us from the truth that we need to connect with.

Weight, and its ups and downs, is more often than not tied to fear. Fear of failure and fear of success both seem to vie for our focus, distracting us from achieving what could be a lot simpler if we shed the uncertainty and the feelings of being unworthy or weak. Failure is part of the journey; there is a lot to be learned in the process of change. There is no magic potion and no perfection. The grace and love for yourself and others, whom you travel with, are what make the journey successful, positive and fruitful. Weight is both symbolically and literally a manifestation of the connection between mind and body, and when we want to make a healthy change, it is the perfect opportunity to delve deeper into that connection and learn more about ourselves.

Confidence and acceptance of who we are, no matter what size or shape, is at the core of dealing with weight and transformation. Your journey has to start there, with self-love and kindness. Weight loss may be your goal, but the motivation must be about making peace with yourself and finding happiness in something larger (no pun intended) than your physical appearance. When you feel that you are lacking something, whether it is money, love, attention or whatever, it's easy for food to become your substitution. Again, fear plays a role, this time when it comes to emptiness. Rather than seek help, people use eating to distract and numb themselves. The universe will take care of "lack"- our circumstances are continually changing, and the pendulum of life is always moving back and forth. But overcoming the fear, and asking for help when you need it, is necessary to get to the root cause of your feelings of lack. Past events can stop us from trusting that there will always be enough. Everything in your life that is "negative" or uncomfortable is just a messenger to tell you something is out of sync.

Achieving health and well-being is a matter of not just looking inward, but connecting with the world and your relationship to it. It's important to stay engaged and create what you want, need, and what you can share with others. If your mind stops moving because you're not creating, we actually start putting on weight in our physical bodies. Both our thinking, and the way we live our lives, become "weighed down" by the extra pounds, isolating us from true connection with ourselves and with others. Changing the way we picture who we are, and breaking down old preconceptions and limitations, is essential for true and ongoing transformation.

The Power of Your Subconscious

Your subconscious is so powerful, and because it is hidden, you tend to neglect the influence it can exercise over you. When you start to unravel the subconscious, remarkable, life-shifting wisdom is revealed. Working with a therapist, or joining a group of people with the same goals, acts as a mirror or a sounding board that you can bounce your thoughts, experiences and beliefs off of. Your perspective - guided by the subconscious - is not always tied to the truth. With the help of people who can give you feedback, you can hear and process information objectively. A clear, new dynamic between weight and consciousness is created in your mind that allows you to transform your life.

When an event happens in your life that has some uncertainty or discomfort around it, you may tend to tag that event as negative. As soon as you do so, that's exactly what it becomes. The best approach is to say "hang on, the reason why this is happening in my life is because I'm not giving attention to something that needs my consideration and care." If you want to lose weight, gain weight, stop smoking or change any pattern, the first step is to practice taking the negative voice out of your thought process. Those defeating messages may be extremely ingrained in your subconscious, yet there is no reason you cannot start chipping away at them.

Are you relinquishing your own power over your life to your subconscious? Are you using food to conceal the issues that you struggle with? Though it may be a difficult concept to accept and to put into practice, you are your own creator. You are producing your own reality by how you think. No matter what we have endured or suffered in the past, the effects of which lie in our subconscious, we all begin each day with a clean slate of possibility. Your life's story and circumstances might lead you to feel defeated and unlucky. Well, the time to use words like "luck" is over. Change takes hard work, and the harder you work, the luckier you get. Believing in sheer chance, and using it to make excuses, is disempowering. Every conscious thought you are having now is creating your next thought.

All the past actions that you ever experienced, even some that you have no awareness of, reside in the subconscious. You can call it karma, or whatever feels appropriate to you. Those subconscious thoughts and feelings can burden and paralyze you. You must balance the books on them, so to speak, and sort out their meaning. Self-awareness is a journey, and you have the authority over your mind to be the person who can heal yourself with help and support, but ultimately, by your own power. Your critical mind will always keep trying to stand in your way. If you consciously know what causes you to do something, it vanishes. Once you have become conscious of the root cause of a behavior, it has to disappear.

Weight is an extremely complex issue. There are so many manifestations of our subconscious mind that add up to overeating and extra pounds. Becoming heavy, or even anorexic or bulimic, is sometimes about punishing your family, and yourself in the process. I once worked with a client who doubted that her husband loved her the way she needed and/or wanted to be loved. She deliberately planned to become overweight to see if he would stick around. And as it turned out, he left her. Now, regardless of what that tells us about her husband, testing him by gaining weight was self-punishing. She needed to explore her issues with love, trust and security and go deeper to get the answer.

It's not uncommon for people to do extreme things to each other, and themselves, in order to get the attention they feel they lack. Their subconscious distorts their needs and obscures the best way to have them met. I've seen people put on weight because they want to be seen, even if in an unhealthy way. I've also worked with people who became severely anorexic because they did not want to be seen (but actually did want acknowledgment and attention, ironically) by literally trying to disappear off the earth. Though these are just some examples of people dealing with weight, they speak to how complex it is as an issue.

The subconscious is not to be feared. It is a storehouse of riches stemming from all kinds of experiences - joyful, painful and everything in-between. It's how we unearth these thoughts, and recognize them, that is the key. If you allow your un-conscious to write the script of your life, you will not live as fully, happily, and in the present as you can and should. The unconscious is fascinating and speaks to all that you have lived, but it need not rule you. Messages, such as "I'm unattractive" or "I'm not deserving" will keep you from all the potential you embody. If you think you're not beautiful, there's the first thing you need to change. You are absolutely beautiful exactly as you are. If you don't believe that, it doesn't matter what anyone else says to try to convince you. It's up to you to embark on a journey of self-love and acceptance that will create the foundation for a new relationship to weight.

The Weighty Issues of Attachment and Addiction

Addiction to food can exist to varying degrees, but any time we eat as a substitution for love or attention, or as self-medication, or as a way to hide, it is an unhealthy dependence and compulsion. As we uncover addiction, attachment to what we think we need to be happy and fulfilled is revealed. Food often symbolizes attachment to so many emotions and things. Once we let go of attachment in all facets of our lives and accept the flow of events that happen to us - no matter if we deem them good or bad - we can start to break free of attachment. Addiction loses its power when there isn't any attachment to fuel it.

Whether you are overeating or under-eating, it's the same thing. You're hurting yourself for something that has happened to you in your past, or you believe happened, that you think was wrong. Through this addiction to food you are punishing either yourself, or in some instances, getting revenge on others. The pattern of addiction, by its very nature, becomes a coping mechanism. The misuse of any substance, food in this case, becomes a normal way of life, and a way to adapt. Food can temporarily calm nerves and numb pain, but the effect is very short-lived. It's a quick fix to deep-seated issues, and it's a fix that doesn't work. In fact, it will almost always make the person feel worse, but the vicious cycle continues and takes on a life of its own.

The first addiction we have is to life, at all costs. After our first breath we begin to form our first attachment—to our mother, the person who can supply all that we need to survive. Your mother provides love, nourishment and security. If you receive all three of these, life will run smoother for you in the long run (though not without a neurosis or two!) If any of those elements are lacking for you as a young child, you are going to be subject to confusion, and possibly sadness, as an adult.

If you felt unloved as a child, you will have a hard time with your self-image. You may see yourself as fat or ugly. The inner voice, that echoes your past, begins to talk to you like this—"you're unlovable and that's why mom or dad didn't give you all that you needed and wanted." Now that you are adult, and can do what you want, your overeating may become a habit as you attempt to fill up that empty space inside of you. One day you look in the mirror and are shocked—and perhaps depressed—at what the overindulgence has done to your body. When you start a diet it's usually too difficult to stick to it because the inner voice that says you're undeserving is stronger than the conscious voice that says you're lovable and is able to declare, "I'm going to lose this weight."

Food addiction and compulsive eating are tools people use to comfort themselves. As long as you have attachments—to the past, to the hurt, to the desires—you will be in a battle. Once you can just let go of attachments and let them pass through you, perspective and joy will come into your consciousness and help you move past addiction. The conscious mind knows the difference between right and wrong, good and bad. It has discernment. The subconscious mind doesn't and just keeps all of your past experiences and feelings stacked up, deep inside. It thinks it's doing you a favor by holding on to all this information! Unless your subconscious mind is involved in your efforts to lose weight, you'll continue on that not-very-merry-go-round of frustration and self-abuse.

Unlike alcohol, cigarettes or gambling, food cannot be completely eliminated from your life in order to combat an addiction to it. Eating, when sensible, is the source of nourishment and life. The path to a healthy connection to food is one of balance and for-giveness. It's essential that fear be replaced with love, whether it's fear of weight gain, relationships, or any other thing or emotion. Normalizing your dynamic with food can resonate in all areas of life. There is no denying how powerful addiction to anything can be. Learning to approach food with a different perspective is no small feat and getting help and support to get there is important. You don't have to go it alone.

Going Deeper - A Proactive Approach to Weight

If you want to shift the way you are living, whether it be the way weight has come to play a role, or any other aspect of your being, you have to visualize what you want your future to hold and make a very powerful affirmation to yourself. You must promise yourself that you will stop looking back to the traumas you may have experienced in a way that doesn't truly address them, but repeats the trauma, over and over. There are people holding on to things, such as "my father didn't love me," even into their 90's! What you need to do with hurt and trauma is to break it down.

Changing something as basic but powerful as your eating habits and weight is work, and results that last don't happen overnight. When it comes to examining the reasons behind problems that you feel hold you back, be very clear. Start by picking one issue in your life right now that is so glaringly obvious that if it shifted, everything would be dramatically different. Healing is about focusing in on something, not trying to clear the slate in one fell swoop and wipe it clean. Change rarely happens that way. It's much more productive to take a single element that is going on in your life that you are constantly stuck with and drill deep down into it, until you strike water.

When we look at weight and the connection to how you were parented, it may be that your mother and father just did what so many others have inadvertently bestowed on their children mixed messages, confusion and guilt. We have to be very careful about how we interact with people, specifically with children since they don't have the same cognitive faculties as adults have. When you are having a bad day and you shout at a child, "Get off those stairs.

I'm sick of you!" what they hear very often is, "I don't love you anymore." If they're getting a lot of that kind of communication in their life, what are the chances they're going to grow up to be healthy, happy and successful people?

Your mind is an incredible computer of information. It cannot, and will not, do anything except what you ask it to do. If you're constantly saying to yourself, "I'm not good enough," your mind is going to say, "You're right. You're not." So when you hear yourself saying, "I'm not good enough," you have to counteract it with "I am good enough . . . I deserve to treat myself well and believe in me." Though going deeper to combat weight issues starts and ends with you, asking for help is part of the process. There are so many resources to help resolve problems and become much more confident, successful, and productive beings. But you cannot be passive about the journey. If you are proactive in your desire to transform your life, the effects will amaze you.

You may think you've touched upon the root causes of your weight issues, but if you are still struggling with weight, you need to go deeper and really examine the triggers that set off overeating. Was food equated with love, comfort and consolation in your house? Have events in your adult life surrounding issues of love brought you back to that dynamic in seeking to comfort yourself? Did you have a sibling that received more attention? Did you want to be seen more, making yourself "bigger?" Does isolating yourself and hiding behind the weight motivate you? Are you using food to suppress negative feelings and/ or memories? What do you feel you are missing in your life and are you attempting (unsuccessfully) to get it from food? Do your best to drop below the level of just general-izing about these themes, whichever relates to you, and unravel your life. Identify the feeling around events and issues in your life. Name them. Accept them.

When you focus in and understand the link between what happened to you in the past, that's when real change begins, because that's when you let it go. If something is still affecting you and showing up as weight, you have not released it. Combating weight is an emotional, psychological and spiritual journey. The body is integrated with the mind and when we separate and disconnect them, we lose our way. Compulsive eating can be seen as a weapon or tool of self-hatred against the body, but food is not an enemy. [Unhealthy eating is when you are feeding your feelings, not your body.] It's the relationship and affinity that your mind has with your whole conscious being that is disrupted when weight is a problem. The goal is alignment and harmony of the energy between our bodies and our minds.

Mindfulness and Mindful Eating

How many of your everyday actions are automatic and based on habit? Do you stop to think "Am I truly hungry?" before you eat? Do you eat on the run, while you are watching television or on the computer? Being aware of our thoughts, feelings, intentions, and activities start with being mindful. Consciousness arises from a connection to the mind that exists in the present and focuses on the creation of new possibilities at any given moment. Developing a mindful approach to eating and food can shift the paradigm of weight issues. Breaking patterns of association, and just pure habit, is the goal to mindful eating. Through self-education, guided therapy, support groups and/or meditations, mindfulness can be used to make a substantial difference in changing the way we think about eating.

Overeating and bingeing thrive on triggers, many of them subconscious. Do you eat as a reaction to something, rather than as an act of nourishment? Eating because you are bored, angry or tired are particularly common phenomena. Have you ever felt you stuffed anger down with food, rather than taking a moment to connect the anger to its source and work through the feeling? When you reach for that cookie, is it because you are bored and don't know what else to do? What exactly is your boredom based on? Are you keeping yourself away from something that could be new and fulfilling, thinking you don't deserve to indulge yourself in an endeavor that could turn out to be satisfying over the long run? How does that bag of chips help with emotions? Not very well, as it turns out.

Mindful eating takes a holistic approach. The focus is not just on weight loss but even more importantly, it looks at how we can control the way we think. Do you find yourself preoccupied with food? The irony of dieting is that it often creates an imbalance in a normal relationship to eating. Many diets, especially ones that are very restrictive, can lay the groundwork for obsessive thoughts about what you can and cannot have. It makes sense that a dynamic like that would just make you crave the restricted foods even more. Once you go off the diet, you have to eat "normally," something the diet has not helped to reinforce. Mindful eating's goal is to integrate food and eating into the whole of your life and to be clear that you are not eating from a place of emotional substitution. Enjoying and truly savoring food is the gift of mindful eating, as is thinking of overall health and happiness. Food doesn't become a bigger part of your life than it should. There is harmony and balance with the other elements of your day.

Exercising what we call "will power" is usually a losing proposition, and the trap of judging yourself as having "no will power" only sets a negative label on your challenge with weight. Why try, you say to yourself, when you have convinced yourself that you are weak? It's not a matter of being stronger or better than the next person struggling with eating issues. It's about awareness - conscious eating and living. How can you know if you are truly hungry or not unless you learn to listen to your body from a connection with your mind? Do you know your body's natural rhythms and feedback? Forgiveness and openness are part of mindful eating. Even when you splurge or overeat during that holiday meal, you allow yourself the beautiful imperfection of the temporary indulgence. Instead of chastising yourself, you enjoy all that you experience, whether it's on the overall plan or not! If that voice inside your head is looking to punish you, there's little chance you'll be able to break free of the weight and food obsession taking control of you.

Do you live in the moment or are you always running toward a future goal, or away from a past that you have labeled a failure? Are you mindful of ALL the moments in your day? Think about your first thoughts upon waking. Do you start the day in the present, giving yourself an affirmation that grounds you? Are you cognizant of the experience of dressing, eating, working, relating to family and friends? Or, are you "somewhere else" in your head for much of the day? If you let worry, fear and anger seep into those present moments, mindfulness goes off the rails. Though thinking about a multitude of emotions and things to do may seem like multi-tasking, you are actually less productive and focused when you are not mindful. Mindfulness needs your full attention.

Life becomes richer with mindfulness. A decadent dessert is great every once in a while, but the amazing abundance of living fully present and in the moment is available all of the time! Once you find an inner place of nourishment where you are not starved for the self-attention you need, you can establish a peaceful, normalized and healthy relationship with food. If you work to become more connected to your thoughts, emotions and physical signs, you can see how they influence your behavior.

Moderation, Self-Love and Making Peace with Weight

Weight and eating issues pose a contradiction that must be unraveled before you can affect real change. Being unhappy with your weight may motivate you to begin a new plan for losing the pounds, but if you are dissatisfied with yourself, your appearance, and your past inability to maintain weight loss and healthy eating patterns, you'll need to look at self-acceptance and love before you can move forward. There might even be a reason why you are meant to hold on to weight at a particular time in your life. Embrace everything about who you are right now, not in some abstract idea of the future. The premise "I will be happy, successful and lovable if I lose weight" is a losing proposition. Though you may feel those extra pounds have influenced so many aspects of your life, you must be grounded in a certain level of confidence about who you are, no matter how you feel about your physical appearance. There has to be balance between acceptance in the present and willingness to change, to combat weight and food issues. If you set up a system of unrealistic expectations and self-punishment for perceived failures, transformation just isn't possible!

If you adopt an attitude of moderation, you lay the groundwork for self-love. Instead of severe and hard-to-follow diet and exercise regimes, taking on a more moderate plan to make smaller, gradual changes and be kind and forgiving to yourself, is much more effective. Look at the long-term, bigger picture of the life you want, and the way you want to modify your eating and weight. "Feast or famine" doesn't work for our diets, or for any aspect of our lives. Changing your relationship to food is about a lifestyle adjustment, and self-love plays an integral role.

We can all take inspiration from one of the core ideas of Buddhism - The Middle Way, which embodies moderation as an overall perspective and practice. When every aspect of our lives is approached with moderation, balance and harmony are achieved. Eating with The Middle Way in mind is the opportunity to exercise this concept every day. Be mindful about avoiding extremes in your thinking and your actions. This will not only help with weight issues, but with all your interactions, relationships and self-confidence. The Middle Way teaches us that everything is interconnected and that there is always "cause and effect." No matter what your belief system is, there are valuable lessons of balance and self-care in these ideas.

Self-love comes from within, and your mind creates the messaging that supports it. The same is true when approaching how you eat. You are the only one who can take care of your body. You choose what you put into it and it's up to you to try to bring moderation into your overall goal. Start by paying attention and be aware. What triggers your hunger? How do you feel when you are eating? What does the food taste like? Notice the consistency, the texture and the flavor. Changing your eating habits and patterns is a matter of changing the way you think. Though physical exercise is an important aspect of weight and overall health, exercising your mind is just as critical. A diet plan should start with a recipe for conscious and positive affirmations, moderation and self-acceptance. As with weight loss, these new ways of thinking don't happen overnight, but with practice and patience, true change is possible.

The term "battling weight" puts an emphasis on the drama and conflict. Looking at changing your relationship to food and eating with a more peaceful approach is a better bet for lasting change.

The same is true when it comes to the personal journey with one's weight. Though eating and weight centers on the individual, remembering our connectedness to one another is key. We are facing the far-reaching societal issues of obesity, mass-marketing of unhealthy food and changing food production. Try looking at the bigger picture and know that you are not alone. Along with support groups that can be very helpful, expand your thoughts to what kinds of changes would be beneficial not just for you, but for your community, and the world. Get involved with healthy eating programs and education, learn about sustainable food projects and participate in the development of more parks, bike paths, nutritious food shops and other beneficial improvements in your neighborhoods.

Practical Advice and Tools - A New Way of Eating, A New Way of Life

Weight often has very little to do with how much you are eating and more to do with whether or not you are living consciously. I've seen people who eat like birds who were physically heavy and others who could eat you out of house and home who were slim! What kind of food choices do you make? When do you eat? Do you move your body enough? Are you engaged in activity, not just physical, but mental and creative? What other health options do you adopt in daily life? Do you sleep enough hours? Too many hours? Is relaxation and/or meditation part of your day?

For ANY problem you want to address, you have to look at the primal motivating factor as to why you might have an issue, and at the same time, take steps to make practical changes and adjustments. What are some of the best ways to start real transformation when it comes to weight and eating?

- Change your thinking when it comes to weight! You must bring your mind and emotions along with you and stop self-defeating patterns. What is "weighing" you down in your subconscious? Commit to doing the work to uncover these issues, and make peace with your body, whatever size or shape it is.

- Make fresh fruits and vegetables, whole grains and plant-based proteins a larger part of your diet. You don't have to eliminate foods (unless there are medical reasons), just cut back on choices that are not as healthy. Eating less meat, salt and refined sugar lowers the risk of heart disease, high blood pressure and cancer. Increasing fiber in your diet will make you feel fuller and more satisfied. Always be aware that the mind, and your past experiences, play a big role in your relationship to food and nourishment in general.

- Enjoy your food. Don't eat quickly or unconsciously. Take time to be mindful. Reconnect with the idea that food is for nourishment and energy. Making sure it tastes good and satisfies you is important, but remember that food is not love or consolation or comfort. Take the emotion out of eating. [And it's very important to remember that food was not created to be used as a form of entertainment as it is today, but only to sustain the body and mind]

- Get in touch with your natural rhythms and cycles. Space meals appropriately. Eat when you are truly hungry and give yourself time to digest properly. Eating late at night, then going to bed, is an example of ignoring the needs of your body to consume, then burn off energy. And don't beat yourself up if you don't always succeed.

- Eat as much fresh food as possible. Cook what you need and avoid large amounts of leftovers, unless you know you will consume them as meals.

- Water, water, water! We all know how vital water is for health and weight control. But are you drinking enough? And, no, soda does not count toward a liquid goal. Soda, in fact, is one of the leading causes of obesity. [Also, drinking a glass of water when you wake up in the morning will increase your metabolism by 24%, helping you to lose weight.]

- Look at what you can do to increase movement and exercise. Changing your diet alone will not help you with weight. Movement increases your metabolism and produces endorphins, which improve mood and motivation. Lack of time becomes an easy excuse for not exercising. Take the stairs instead of the elevator. Park a little bit away from where you are going. Replace a family drive with a bike ride in nature. There are plenty of low-impact exercise choices, such as yoga or tai chi, so your physical capabilities and limitations don't have to be a deterrent.

- Above all, health is your objective. Being skinny is not! Your body has its natural set point, within the range of good health. Accepting who you are also includes knowing your body. It should function optimally, with energy, freedom from strain and pain, and the absence of health-threatening conditions. What you weigh is not important if you are working toward those goals.

Meditations and Exercises for Mindful Eating

A mantra for losing weight: "I am losing weight easily, effortlessly and naturally."

A mantra for gaining weight: "I am gaining healthy weight easily, effortlessly and naturally."

Visualize yourself wearing the clothes that would fit after you succeed in your goal. See yourself the size you would be after achieving your goal. See yourself doing more energetic types of activities after you've achieved your goal. See yourself enjoying salads without dressing to feel the natural vibration of the food.

ABOUT THE AUTHOR

For more than 20 years, Derek O'Neill has been transforming the lives of thousands of people around the world for the better. An internationally acclaimed transformational coach and therapist, motivational speaker, author, martial arts sensei and humanitarian, Derek inspires and uplifts people from all walks of life through his workshops, consultations, speaking engagements, media, and tireless humanitarian work.

Drawing on thirty years of training in martial arts, which earned him the level of Master Black Belt, coupled with his extraordinary intuitive abilities and expertise as a psychotherapist, Derek has pioneered a new psychology, transformational therapy. His signature process, aptly named "The Sword and the Brush," helps clients to seamlessly transmute their struggles into positive outcomes, using the sword to cut away old patterns and the brush to help paint the picture of the new life that they require.

In addition to reaching large audiences through workshops and media, Derek advises individuals, celebrities, business leaders, and politicians, helping them to find new perspectives on long-standing issues and bringing harmony back to their lives and businesses.

Author of More Truth Will Set You Free, the Get a Grip series of pocket books, a cutting edge book on parenting titled Calm Mama,

Happy Baby, and several children's books, Derek also hosted his own radio show, "The Way With Derek O'Neill," which enjoyed the most successful launch in VoiceAmerica's history, quickly garnering 100,000 listeners.

Derek is a master at offering practical wisdom and proven techniques for living a more harmonious and fulfilling life, bringing CEOs to the level of wise yogi and wise yogis to CEO; he has worked with executives from some of the world's major airlines, and the cast of Spiderman on Broadway to help transform group disharmony and untapped creative potential into productivity and dynamic performance. He has been featured in Exceptional People Magazine, The Irish Independent, The Irish Examiner, CBS television, and RTE, Ireland's national TV network.

Inspired by his worldly travels, he formed SQ Foundation, a not-for-profit organization focused on helping to solve global issues facing humanity today. In 2012, he was honored as Humanitarian of the Year and named International Celebrity Ambassador for Variety International the Children's Charity. He was welcomed as Vice President of the esteemed charity in May 2013.

Recordings of Derek's discourses are available for download, offering practical wisdom and proven techniques for living a more harmonious and fulfilling life.

To learn more about Derek O'Neill, to attend his next workshop, to order books, downloads or to contact him, please visit his website:

derekoneill.com

To learn more about SQ Foundation, the global charity that is changing the lives of hundreds of thousands of people around the world, go to:

sq-foundation.org

MORE RESOURCES FROM DEREK O'NEILL

Videos, Audio Downloads, Live Broadcasts, Books, Blog and more at **derekoneill.com**

Get a Grip Book Series

Happiness: You Must Be Effin' Joking!

Anger: Who Gives a Shite?

Relationships: Would You Want to Date You?

Depression: What's that?

Weight: What's Eating You?

Confidence: Easy For You to Say

Abundance: Starts Right Now

Fear: A Powerful Illusion

Addiction: What a Cover-Up!

Excellence: You Never Lost It, You Forgot It

Grief: Mind Boggling But Natural

Suicide: Fast or Slow

Stress: Is Stress Stressing You Out?

Dreams: The Best Messengers

Mindfulness: Out Of Or In Your Mind?

Forgiveness: So I Can Move On

Books

More Truth Will Set You Free

Calm Mama, Happy Baby

Children's Books

Water Drop Coloring Book

The Adventures of Lucinda in Love-Filled Fairyland

SOCIAL MEDIA

YouTube

youtube.com/DerekONeill101

Facebook

facebook.com/DerekONeill101

Twitter

twitter.com/DerekONeill101

LinkedIn

linkedin.com/in/DerekONeill101